# ABOVE PARIS

by ROBERT CAMERON

A new collection of aerial
photographs of Paris, France

with text by
PIERRE SALINGER

Cameron and Company, San Francisco, California

MAINTENON

(Opposite) VAUX-LE-VICOMTE

## TABLE OF CONTENTS

Such a book as this does not reach publication without more than the usual amount of cooperation from many people. So, for their encouragement and expertise we thank the following:

Francois Benoist, Guy Buffet, Robert Burger, Todd Cameron, Ken Cellini, Jean-Louis Clément, Phillippe-Marie Denis, Michel Drucker, Mary Foster, Yves Groetschel, Alice Harth, Suzanne Lawlor, Mary Martinet, Patricia O'Grady, Dolly Patterson, Julian Peabody, Gilbert Rosati, Eric Steinle, and Henry Struck.

Helicopter Pilot Patrick Le Boedec of Professional Air System, Jean Créon Mgr.

And for very special expertise and talent
both on the ground and in the air, Josebeth Drucker.

CAMERON AND COMPANY

543 Howard Street   San Francisco, California 94105   415/777-5582

First Printing, 1984

©1984 by Robert W. Cameron and Company. All rights reserved.
Library of Congress Catalog Number: 84-071415
Above Paris ISBN 0-918684-19-6

Book design by
JANE OLAUG KRISTIANSEN

Typography by Reeder Type Inc.   Color film processing by Colortec, Paris   Color Separation and Printing by Dai Nippon Printing Co., Tokyo, Japan
Cameras: Pentax 6x7 System

# FOREWORD—ABOVE PARIS

I first came to Paris in December of 1925. My mother decided it was a good occasion to have me baptized as a Catholic. She chose, not just any church, but Notre-Dame Cathedral. I was six months old at the time, but my feelings about Paris today lead me to believe that there must be some kind of osmosis at work in the being of a young child. Otherwise, why would Paris continue to haunt me long after as a place I wanted to see, and where eventually I wanted to live?

I returned to Paris almost 36 years later, to help advance President Kennedy's visit to France soon after his election. I will never forget the impact the city made on me the day I landed in April of 1961. I had the feeling I had arrived, not just in a city, but in a living museum, reflecting 23 centuries of history.

Finally, in 1968, after Robert Kennedy was killed, this second tragedy of the Kennedys in my life in 5 years, I felt the need to get away from America for a while. The logical choice was Paris. I have been here ever since.

In November of 1983 I made a brief trip to San Francisco to give some lectures at my alma mater, the University of San Francisco, and it was at that time that I met Bob Cameron. He had just finished *Above Yosemite*, a stunning work on one of the most beautiful regions of the United States. It was the culmination of a series of "Above" books—San Francisco, Los Angeles, Hawaii, Washington, D.C., and London. He told me he wanted to do *Above Paris*, and asked if I would work with him. I immediately said yes. Yet there were unexpected problems. Over the past two decades security has been considerably tightened in Paris. Authorization to fly above the city in a helicopter is one of the things it is almost impossible to obtain. But I tried. In January of 1984 I had my first appointment with the Préfet de Police, Guy Fougier, to apply for the necessary permissions. I took with me a copy of

*Above London*, as my best argument. M. Fougier was enthusiastic about the idea, but even with the power he had to grant authorization, he admitted it would be very difficult.

By April, however, the Prefecture was so encouraging that I advised Bob to come to Paris. Throughout the month, Paris had some of the most beautiful weather it has ever seen in April. Finally, at the end of the month, our authorization came—but for just a single hour of flight at from 1,200 to 2,000 feet, depending on the location. If that were not discouraging enough, now another factor intervened: the weather turned sour. Bob took what photographs he could, and returned home. It seemed that *Above Paris* was doomed.

I soon discovered, however, that Bob had not wasted his time. During his stay he had taken a helicopter to the château-rich section outside of Paris. And in the brief half-hour over Paris he had gotten some stunning shots of the capital. We decided to make a mock-up of the book with what he had. There was still a way to get authorization for the critical photographs we needed.

The mock-up arrived in Paris on June 4, and the following day I had an invitation to lunch with some high government officials. We were only eight around the table, so that after lunch I had a few moments to show them the proposed book and to explain our problem. They were taken with the project and agreed to instruct the proper authorities with the permissions. The authorizations were received within 48 hours. This time Bob would be allowed to fly at a lower altitude to give his eye and his camera a clearer view of Paris.

The result is glowing, for Paris in its entirety has never been seen quite like this. The Ile de la Cité with its imposing Cathedral, the familiar but ever new Eiffel Tower, the modern Pompidou Center in its bright blue and red standing in the

middle of an historic and traditional neighborhood, the Arc de Triomphe and the Champs-Elysées—all are seen here in an entirely new dimension, and they add a new perspective to France's capital. This unique photographic collection reflects the long history of France, going back three centuries before Christ, through years of war and revolution, to the time when it became the cultural center of the world, an intellectual beacon to artists, musicians, architects, scientists from around the globe. One can understand why virtually every modern American composer came to Paris to do their early work, why writers like Ernest Hemingway, Scott Fitzgerald and Henry Miller made Paris their home. That ancient Paris has little changed, although it has acquired a bit of modern look with the skyscraper complex at La Défense, the high rise office buildings, apartments and hotels on the banks of the Seine, and the towering Tour Montparnasse, the tallest building in Paris, opened in 1973.

From the window of my apartment on the Rue de Rivoli the view is like a living history book. Looking from left to right, I can see Notre-Dame Cathedral, the Louvre, the Jeu de Paume, the church of Sainte Clothilde, the National Assembly, the Dome of the Invalides, the Tuileries Gardens, the Grand Palais, and the Eiffel Tower. In seeing this panorama of Gothic, Renaissance, and modern structures, one relives the times of kings and empire, the Revolution of 1789, the uprising of the Paris Commune of 1871, the two world wars and the spectacular liberation of Paris of August 25, 1944, the student uprisings of May of 1968. But one also sees the neighborhoods that became the paintings of Toulouse-Lautrec, of Monet and Manet, and the inspiration of artists like Picasso and Chagall. Paris is the city of wonder. This book consecrates that wonder.

PIERRE SALINGER
Paris, July 8, 1984

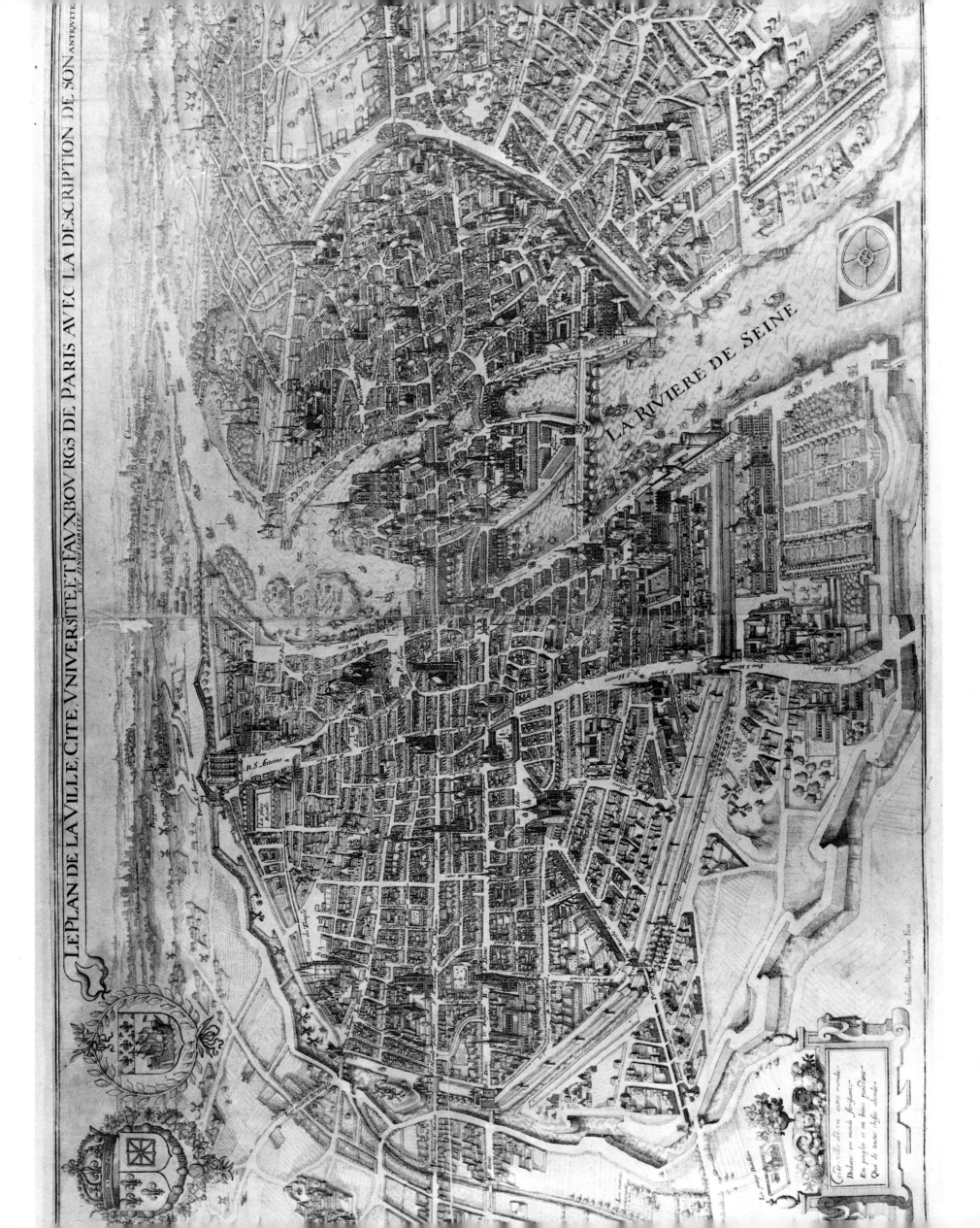

LE PLAN DE LA VILLE, CITE, VNIVERSITE ET TAVXBOVRGS DE PARIS, AVEC LA DESCRIPTION DE SON ANTIQVITE ET SINGVLARITES

LA RIVIERE DE SEINE

# BIRD'S-EYE PERSPECTIVE, HISTORICAL AND MODERN

CITY PLAN OF PARIS DRAWN IN 1615

On the left is a city plan of Paris drawn in 1615. In the middle of the Seine, one can see the Ile de la Cité, with the Notre-Dame Cathedral, the Palais de la Justice, and the Conciergerie. Behind the Ile de la Cité are two small uninhabited islands which have been joined and are now the fashionable Ile St. Louis. In the background, on the left, is the prison of La Bastille, assaulted by mobs on July 14, 1789, at the beginning of the French Revolution. On the right is a view of the islands of the Seine.

On this page is a reproduction of the first aerial photograph ever taken. It was made by the famous Nadar, in 1854, who worked from a balloon. He is shown here in its basket. On the opposite page, is the same area, after 130 years of expansion.

PARYS

In the beginning of the seventeenth century, after a series of epidemics of the plague, a decision was made to build a new hospital. It was constructed outside the walls of Paris to protect the citizens from contagion. This mid-seventeenth century drawing shows the Hospital St. Louis along with its beautiful chapel. On the right, now well within the city, is the same hospital, which continues to be an important medical center.

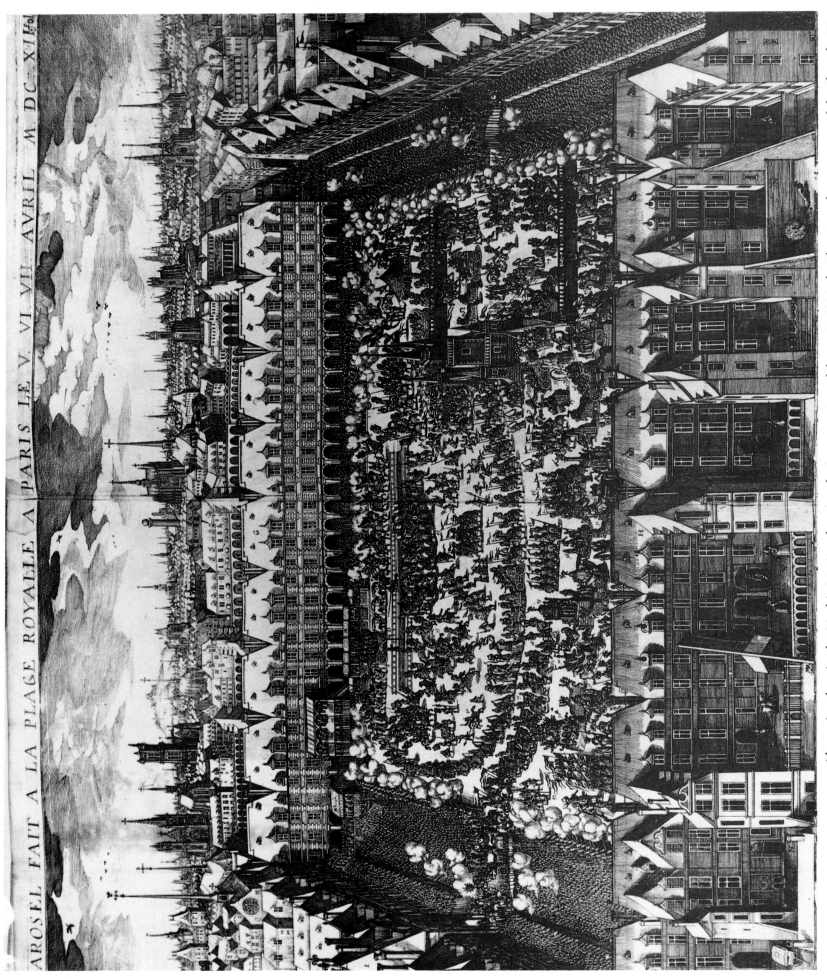

Above, is a drawing by Mathie Merian showing the inauguration of the Place Royale in April of 1612. The Place is filled with musicians, cavaliers, and an enormous crowd which came to celebrate a double marriage—that of King Louis XIII and that of his sister. The Place Royale was situated in the heart of the Marais, then Paris' most fashionable neighborhood where aristocrats, royalty, and the rich financiers built opulent homes. There was a period when the Marais was abandoned to small artisans, but, recently, many of the old homes have been restored.

In 1800, the Place Royale was renamed the Place des Vosges. In the photo on the right, one can see how little the old Place Royale has changed, how the old buildings, which surround the square, still reflect their historic past. On the lower left side of the photo, we see one of the fashionable homes of the seventeenth century, the Hôtel de Bethune Sully, purchased in 1634 by Maximilien de Bethune, Duke of Sully, a former minister of Henri IV.

PORTRAIT DV MAGNIFIQVE BASTIMENT DE LA MAISON DE VILLE·DE PARIS·

Mathieu Matian's engraving of the Hotel de Ville (City Hall) of Paris was made in 1645 during the Feast of Saint Jean. Jacques Hilairet wrote, "The Hotel de Ville of Paris has been the palace of all the revolutions; the rallying place for all national emotions. To tell its history is to tell the history of the nation."

The first municipality of Paris was created in 1246 and in 1357 it was moved into a building on this same site. The version in the drawing was built during the reign of Francois I by an Italian architect known as le Boccador. In May 1871, the Hotel de Ville in the engraving was destroyed during the Commune.

The new Hotel de Ville, constructed between 1873 and 1883, seen in the photograph on the right, is a copy of the previous version. The mayor of Paris, Jacques Chirac, whose offices are here, was elected by universal suffrage in 1977. On the upper right of the photograph, one can see the tip of the Ile de la Cité, and in the upper middle of the picture is the beginning of the Ile Saint Louis.

18

PLAN PERSPECTIF DE L'ÉCOLE ROYALE MILITAIRE

In 1778, the French artist, Lespinasse, did this drawing of the Ecole Royale Militaire. On the right, one can see how things have changed. The same area, seen from the air, shows one stupendous difference; that is, the presence of the Eiffel Tower, which was inaugurated in 1889 during the Universal Exposition of that year. The Ecole Royale Militaire, which was constructed in the mid-eighteenth century still stands as one of France's most beautiful architectural creations. Between it and the Eiffel Tower are the lovely trees and gardens of the Champ de Mars, the site of huge demonstrations during the Revolution and site of the first launching of a hydrogen balloon in 1783.

20

## DRAWING OF TUILERIES

Above, is an early nineteenth century drawing of the Tuileries Gardens dominated by the Palais des Tuileries, which was built in the sixteenth century by Catherine di Médici. The royal castle was destroyed during the uprising of the Paris Commune in 1871. All that remains today are the two

pavillons on the left and on right sides of the château, the Pavillon de Flore, and the Pavillon de Marsan. Behind the royal castle one can see the Louvre and the Place du Carousel, which, at one time, was filled with private homes. On the right is a view of the Tuileries Gardens.

ASPECT GÉNÉRAL DE PARIS.

PRISE À VOL D'OISEAU DE L'ENTRÉE DES CHAMPS ÉLYSÉES.

(Opposite) This is an unusual picture of the Place de la Concorde in that scaffolding is rising from the center to provide reviewing stands for the Bastille Day celebration on July 14.

PLACE DE LA BASTILLE

It was here in the Place de la Bastille that the French Revolution was born. The Bastille, a prison finished in 1382, was assaulted by a mob on July 14, 1789. It was soon captured, its prisoners were freed, and the building was destroyed. But, the Place de la Bastille has remained the gathering point for protest and celebration by popular factions in France.

In the middle of the Place, a 171-foot column was erected in memory of the Parisians killed in July of 1830. There was a huge mob here on May 10, 1981, when President François Mitterand was elected. With him, he brought the French left to power.

24

CONCORDE, CHAMPS ELYSEES
Above, an 1865 drawing of the Champs Elysées. In the foreground, the end of the Tuileries Gardens and the Place de la Concorde. At right, the same view but shot from a little farther away.

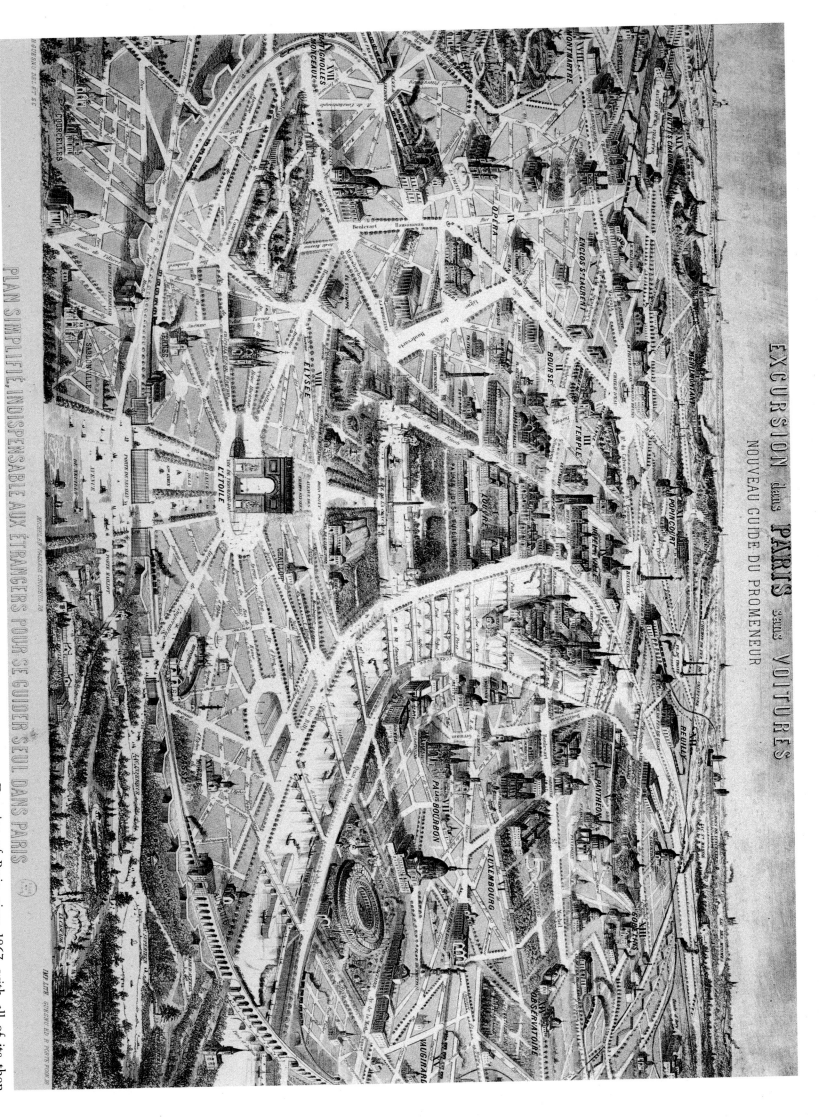

Drawing of Paris, circa 1867, with all of its then famous landmarks identified.

LE PREMIER KILOMÈTRE BOUCLÉ EN AEROPLANE

Le prix Deutsch-Archdeacon de 50.000 francs gagné par M. Henri Farman sur le champ de manœuvres d'Issy-les-Moulineaux : instantané pris au moment du retour de l'aviateur entre les poteaux d'arrivée

Above, is a photo of the British pilot, Henri Farman, son of the Paris correspondent of the London newspaper, *The Standard*. Farman made one of the first flights, in 1908, at Issy-les-Moulineaux. The flight (the first specific "point-to-point") lasted one minute and twenty-eight seconds and covered a little over 1,000 yards at about 30 miles per hour. On the right is the Paris heliport which is in Issy-les-Moulineaux, on the west end of Paris. It is from here that we flew to photograph *Above Paris*.

## POMPIDOU CENTER

The George Pompidou Center, a modern and extremely colorful addition to one of Paris' more traditional neighborhoods, has attracted massive crowds. Heavily criticized at first, as was the Eiffel Tower when it was built, the Pompidou Center has now taken its place as one of the French capital's most popular attractions. At the front of the Center is a large piazza constantly filled with mimes, fire-eaters, jugglers, and street musicians. The Center includes the National Museum of Modern Art,

the Public Information Library, the Industrial Design Center, and the Institute of Acoustic and Musical Research (IRCAM), where new technology and music are combined. The Center was opened in 1977, three years after President George Pompidou, who created the idea, died. Above, is a photo taken in 1951, which shows the demolition that was necessary to make room for the Pompidou Center.

RUNGIS

Paris' giant wholesale produce market, has been located near Orly Airport since 1969. Before that, (above) the produce market, called Les Halles, was located in the center of Paris in ten giant halls, designed by the architect, Baltard, and built between 1854 and 1866. Two other halls were added in 1936.

But, pick-up and delivery trucks caused such traffic jams in modern Paris, that it was necessary to move the market out of the city. The lower color photograph shows the former Les Halles area as it looks today.

# INSIDE THE PERIPHERIQUE

## ILE SAINT-LOUIS AND ILE DE LA CITE

This is an overall view of two historic islands in the Seine, the Ile Saint-Louis, in the foreground, and, in the background, the Ile de la Cité, the historic cradle of Paris. It was here, in the third century B.C., that the Parisii tribe settled, thus beginning the Gallo-Roman Period and the founding of the city of Paris. Today, the Ile de la Cité contains Notre-Dame Cathedral and the complex of the Palais de Justice.

Both Islands are linked to the left and to the right banks of the Seine by a series of bridges, some built as early as the seventeenth century. On the Ile Saint Louis, there remain some sumptuous houses, for example, the Hôtel Lambert built in 1640.

PONT DES ARTS–PONT NEUF

(Opposite) In the foreground is the Pont des Arts, a pedestrian bridge which cuts across the Seine from the Louvre to the French Institute. Behind the Pont des Arts, cutting across the Seine and the Ile de la Cité, is the Pont Neuf, which, despite its name meaning "new bridge," is the oldest bridge in Paris, dating back to 1578. In the background, stands Notre-Dame Cathedral.

PLACE DAUPHINE–ACADEMIE FRANCAISE

This little piece of land between the complex of the Palais de Justice and the tip of the Ile de la Cité is called the Place Dauphine. It was the idea of Henri IV, in the beginning of the seventeenth century, to build a triangular park in honor of the Dauphin (the heir apparent to the throne) who became Louis XIII.

In the background, on the right, are the French Institute and the headquarters of the French Academies which honor the best in writing, science, the arts, and political sciences. Before his death in 1661, Cardinal Mazarin bequeathed the money to build a college for sixty students. But, after the Revolution, Napoléon transformed the building into headquarters for the Institute. The most known of the Academies is the Académie Francaise, with only forty members, the majority of whom are writers. When one dies, the remaining members elect the successor. There has been only one woman admitted to the Academy, Marguerite Yourcenar. The Institute also includes Cardinal Mazarin's rich and extensive library. 37

## CONCORDE-MADELEINE

The Place de la Concorde, in the foreground, Paris' largest square, an area of twenty-one acres, is replete with history. Originally, it was named after Louis XV, and a statue was placed there to honor the King. The statue was torn down and destroyed in 1792, during the French Revolution, and the guillotine was installed there.

In 1836, in the middle of the Concorde, Louis-Philippe erected an ancient obelisk from Luxor, Egypt, given to France by Mehemet-Ali, the Viceroy of Egypt. The obelisk continues to occupy its original place. It was on the Place de la Concorde that Louis XVI, Marie-Antoinette, Robespierre, and more than a thousand other persons were decapitated.

## RUE DE RIVOLI

In the foreground is the Rue de Rivoli, one of Napoléon's projects, which was finished in the middle of the nineteenth century. Seen below and above an arcade are a succession of buildings uniformly designed in the Empire style. Behind the Rue de Rivoli, one can see the Place Vendôme, with the Rue de la Paix and its fancy jewelry shops, such as Cartier, running north out of the Place. On the right, in the rear, is the Paris Opera.

## RUE DE RIVOLI AND PLACE VENDÔME

The Rue de Rivoli was built between 1800 and 1835. Its north side is the most cohesive example in Paris of the architecture inspired by the French Empire. Across the street from these majestic buildings, which are mostly apartments, are located the Louvre and the Tuileries Gardens. Behind the Rue de Rivoli is the famed Place Vendôme, which was first established at the end of the seventeenth century. There stood the statue of Louis XIV, which was destroyed during the Revolution and re-

placed by the famed Vendôme column made up of 1,200 melted cannons seized in battle by Napoléon in 1805 from the Russians and the Austrians. The column was erected in honor of the soldiers who won the Battle of Austerlitz. It was torn down during the Paris Commune in 1871 but was put up again in 1873. This time, a statue of Napoléon I, dressed as a Roman Emperor, was placed on top of the column.

41

42

NOTRE-DAME

It has been said of Notre-Dame: "It is not the highest, largest, or richest church, but, there is none more perfect." Construction of the Cathedral started in 1163, and Pope Alexander III laid the first stone. The construction took only seventy-five years, which was exceptional for that time. Since then, Notre-Dame has been intimately linked with the history of

France. Napoléon was proclaimed Emperor there in 1804. The Cathedral was badly damaged during the Revolution. It was not until 1845 that Viollet-le-Duc undertook seventeen years of restoration work. Behind Notre-Dame, one can see the Préfecture de Police, Paris' police headquarters, located like the Cathedral, on the Ile de la Cité.

THE GRAND PALAIS AND THE PETIT PALAIS

(Opposite) The Grand Palais and the Petit Palais were built for the Paris Universal Exposition of 1900. At the left side of the Grand Palais is the Palais de la Découverte, a center for scientific instruction. It includes scientific exhibits and a planetarium. The Grand Palais and the Petit Palais are today the sites for prestigious art and other types of exhibits.

ROND-POINT DES CHAMPS-ELYSEES

The Rond-Point des Champs-Elysées was designed in 1670 by the famed French architect of gardens, André Le Nôtre. At that time, the Rond-Point was one end of the Champs-Elysées, which only ran to the Place Royale, the Concorde of today. But, in the eighteenth century, the Champs-Elysées was lengthened to reach the Etoile, where the Arc de Triomphe now stands.

FRONT DE SEINE

Some of the modern apartment buildings, office blocks, and hotels, which have recently sprung up on the left bank of the Seine River, can be seen in this photograph. Behind them is the Eiffel Tower. Also evident, are the roofs of the Grand Palais, the Petit Palais, and the Church of the Madeleine.

EIFFEL TOWER

(Opposite) Built for the Universal Exposition of 1889, the Eiffel Tower is the creation of the engineer, Gustave Eiffel, who also built the metalwork for the interior of the Statue of Liberty. Artists and intellectuals of the time attacked the project as "useless and monstrous." But, today, it remains Paris' number one tourist attraction. The Eiffel Tower, which is more than 1000 feet high since television relays were added, is composed of 15,000 pieces of metal and 2,500,000 rivets. In 1982 and 1983, the Eiffel Tower was refurbished and now contains an elegant restaurant, the Jules Verne. To the left of the Eiffel Tower is the Champ-de-Mars. Behind it, across the Seine, is the Maison de la Radio, headquarters of Radio France.

## THE INVALIDES

(Opposite) The Invalides, one of the most spectacular points of interest in Paris, was originally the work of Louis XIV, who had it built between 1671 and 1676 as a barracks for 4,000 wounded soldiers. It was here, on July 14, 1789, that the mob first attacked. They overpowered the guards and took almost 30,000 rifles for the assault on the Bastille, which launched the French Revolution. Here the body of Napoleon was returned in 1840. His remains were kept under the Cupola until a specially-designed tomb was ready in 1861.

The famed Esplanade, in front, was constructed between 1704 and 1720. It is almost 600 yards long and 300 yards wide. In the back of the Invalides are the Church of Saint-Louis-des-Invalides and the Dome Church, also constructed under the reign of Louis XIV. In 1937, 350,000 sheets of gold were used to gild the dome. The total weight of the gold was only fourteen pounds.

## SEMINAIRE DES MISSIONS ETRANGERES

The Seminaire des Missions Etrangères was first built in the seventeenth century. It still exists in the same building with its vast and original gardens. This area is only one example of the hidden gardens which dot Paris. These are, for the most part, unknown to people in the street, because they cannot see past the walls or the building fronts which hide them.

## MUSEE RODIN

The building, which houses the Rodin Museum, was constructed in 1728. Marshall de Biron purchased the structure, and it became the Hôtel Biron. After Marshall de Biron's death, just before the Revolution, the house served a series of functions: as a dance hall, as the headquarters of the Papal legation, and as the residence of the Ambassador of the Tsar.

In 1904, the buildings at the rear of the garden were converted to a grammar school. The house was made available to artists. The celebrated French sculptor, Auguste Rodin, lived there until his death in 1917, after which it was converted to a museum in his honor. The gardens were restored to their eighteenth century design. On the left of the photograph is the Invalides.

## PLACE DE LA RÉPUBLIQUE

Situated in the working class district of Paris, the Place de la République has, at its center, a monument to the French Republic, created by the sculptor, Morice, and erected in 1883. On the right, the Verines Barracks was built in 1854 to house 2,000 men. Most of the important labor demonstrations take place in marches between the Bastille and the Place de la République.

MAISON DE LA RADIO

The Maison de la Radio, built in 1963, houses all of the different elements of Radio France, the state-owned radio network. The interior of the building, which includes concert halls, is a veritable maze, as difficult to navigate as the Pentagon.

ST. GERVAIS

(Opposite) This is a rather wide-angle shot of the modern and colorful Pompidou Center which stands in the middle of the Beaubourg section of Paris. In the foreground are the City Hall and the Hôtel de Ville. In the back, in the center, is the Church of St. Gervais St. Protais which has stood on this site since the sixteenth century. This form of architecture extended from the fifteenth to the seventeenth centuries. The classical facade of this church was the first one built in Paris.

THE CLUNY MUSEUM
(Opposite) What is now the Cluny Museum was built on a site which was occupied, in the third century, by a Gallo-Roman public bath. The site was purchased in the early fourteenth century by the Abbot of Cluny, who built a residence there and transformed it, in 1500, to its present design. The Museum was founded after the French Revolution and is devoted to art of the Middle Ages. It is fascinating to see some of the remains of the public baths.

THE MOSQUE
The Mosque of Paris, dominated by a minaret, was built just after World War I. Paris' Moslem population has grown considerably in the last fifty years, particularly through the influx of immigrant workers from North Africa. In the background, are the Botanical Gardens.

55

## THE MONTSOURIS PARK

The Montsouris Park, planned and completed between 1868 and 1878, has a replica of the home of the Bey of Tunis, which was offered to the city for the 1867 Exposition. The Park has continuously attracted many painters. The famed Georges Braque lived in an apartment bordering the park.

## THE PANTHÉON

(Opposite) The Panthéon, built at the direction of Louis XV, was started in 1758 as the church for the Sainte-Geneviève cloister. Sainte-Geneviève is the religious patron of Paris. The church was not finished until 1789. In 1791, the revolutionary leaders decided that the Panthéon should house the ashes of the great figures of French history. Voltaire, Jean-Jacques Rousseau, and Victor Hugo are there. Included also is Jean Moulin, a hero of the French resistance, killed by the Germans during World War II. In the foreground is one of Paris' highest-rated secondary schools, the Lycee Henri IV, located in what remains of the cloister.

**UNESCO**

The modern building in the foreground is the headquarters of UNESCO, the United Nations Educational, Scientific, and Cultural Organization. On the left is the Ecole Militaire.

58

## UNIVERSITE PIERRE ET MARIE CURIE

Seen from above the Seine is the Université Pierre et Marie Curie. Its tower partly obscures the Place Jussieu. Beyond and to the right is the Arènes de Lutèce.

## ST-GERMAIN-DES-PRES

(Opposite) The Boulevard St. Germain runs through the historic left bank of the Seine, district of St.-Germain-des-Prés, once a farming area outside Paris. St.-Germain-des-Prés became the site of aristocratic mansions of pre-revolutionary times. Before and after World War II, it was the favorite hangout of the Parisian and foreign intelligentsia.

Now a popular place for students and tourists, it is dotted with small cafés and bistros. The area is also filled with beautiful churches.

## THE VAL-DE-GRACE

The Val-de-Grâce, the Abbey and Church of which were built in the seventeenth century, is now a medical center and a site for higher education. The Val-de-Grâce includes a museum devoted to military medicine.

## PALAIS-ROYAL

Little remains today of the original Palais-Royal, the work of Cardinal de Richelieu in the seventeenth century. From him, it passed into the hands of royalty. In 1661, Moliere and his troupe played in a theater in the Palais-Royal. Just before the Revolution, Philippe d'Orleans built 60 pavilions around three sides of the Palais, which later became boutiques. After the Revolution, the Palais was turned into a gambling and dancing hall. In 1836, it was closed. Today, it houses only the Conseil d'Etat (the Council of State) and the Ministry of Culture. The gardens of the Palais were designed in the eighteenth century.

## THE LOUVRE

(Opposite) The Louvre is the largest and one of the most extraordinary palaces in the world. It started as a fortress around the year 1200. The buildings of today's actual Louvre were started in 1546 under Francois I. Construction proceeded during the following years under a succession of monarchs. The final work was done by Napoleon III. After the French Revolution, the Convention decided to turn the Louvre into a museum. At that time, it contained 650 art objects; today, the number is 400,000. It has one of the most valuable art collections in the world.

In 1564, Catherine de Medici started to build a castle opposite the Louvre and between it and the Place de la Concorde of today. But her Tuileries Palace was destroyed during the uprising of the Paris Commune in 1871. As a result, there is now an exceptionally straight line which exists between the Louvre and the Arc de Triomphe and which passes through the garden of the Tuileries, the Place de la Concorde, and the Champs Elysées.

SAINT-SULPICE
(Opposite) Saint-Sulpice was once a parish church for the peasants living outside Paris in Saint-Germain des Prés. It was constructed in the sixteenth, seventeenth and eighteenth centuries. On the far right, you can see the Palais du Luxembourg, the seat of the French Senate.

THE SORBONNE
The Sorbonne, the most prestigious institution of higher education in France, is situated on the left bank of the Seine. It was originally founded in the mid-thirteenth century as a school for poor students. The construction of the present complex was directed by Cardinal de Richelieu in the seventeenth century. Suppressed by the Revolution, the Sorbonne and the University of Paris were reopened by Napoleon. Extensive rebuilding and additions to the complex took place at the end of the nineteenth century and at the beginning of the twentieth century.

The Sorbonne was the center of the student riots in May, 1968. These riots, which paralyzed France, became known as the "Events of May" and led to an extensive reform of the French system of higher education. The Sorbonne Church, in the center, was erected between 1635 and 1642. The tomb of Cardinal de Richelieu is in the church.

## THE PALAIS DU LUXEMBOURG

The Palais du Luxembourg was bult in the early seventeenth century for Marie di Medici, the widow of Henri IV, and was decorated with large paintings by Rubens. These works are now in the Louvre. The palace remained with the royal family until the Revolution when it was converted to a prison. Since 1800, it has been the site of the upper house of the French Legislature, named the Senate in 1852 by Napoléon III. On the left is the Petit Luxembourg, the home of the President of the Senate. The expansive gardens at the rear of the palace were also designed during the time of Marie di Medici.

## THE ARCHIVES

(Opposite) Soon after the French Revolution, the historic Archives of France were placed in the Hôtel Soubise (in the foreground). Built in 1705, the hotel also contains the Historical Museum of France. The Hôtel de Rohan (behind the Hôtel Soubise) became an annex for the Archives in 1927.

66

GARE MONTPARNASSE—TOUR MONTPARNASSE

Rising 688 feet from behind one of Paris' most important railroad stations is the Tour Montparnasse. Completed in 1973, it is the tallest building in Paris. From the restaurant and bar on the 56th floor, there is a spectacular view of Paris. On the left, in the rear, one can see the Invalides.

THE OBSERVATORY

The four walls of the Observatory, constructed in 1667, are oriented to the points of the compass. Within the Observatory are the International Time Bureau, which sets Coordinated Universal Time, and a speaking clock, which can be reached by telephone. This clock is accurate to one-fiftieth of a second. In the background is the Palais du Luxembourg, the seat of the French Senate.

ECOLE MILITAIRE

The Ecole Militaire (military school), completed in 1772, now houses a number of the higher schools of French National Defense and schools of Advanced War Studies attended by French and allied officers. On the right is another view of the Ecole Militaire with the Invalides in the background.

SAINT-SÉVERIN AND SAINT-JULIEN-LE-PAUVRE

(Opposite) The church of Saint-Séverin was begun in the sixth century. It became a parish church for the left bank of the Seine in the eleventh century, when the area was mostly farmland. The present Gothic church, on this same site, was begun in the middle of the thirteenth century.

On the bottom, at the right, is the church of Saint-Julien-le-Pauvre, which has been located here since the third century. The present building, which replaced the old church, was constructed between the twelfth and thirteenth centuries.

BOULEVARD SAINT-GERMAIN

In the seventh arrondissement at lower right, we get a glimpse of the National Assembly and above it is Saint-Clotilde. At center, the modern building is the Ministry of Defense in the Boulevard Saint-Germain.

73

## NATIONAL ASSEMBLY

The National Assembly, the lower house of the French Legislature, is installed in an historic building called the Palais Bourbon. The original building on the property was built in the early eighteenth century by the Duchess of Bourbon, a daughter of Louis XIV. It was enlarged and embellished during the reigns of Louis XV and Louis XVI. The Palace was confiscated during the Revolution and used as a meeting place for the Council of 500.

In 1827, the palace was converted to its present function, as the home of the National Assembly. Made up of 491 members, the National Assembly has virtually all of the legislative power in France. Very little power is in the hands of the Senate, as it cannot stop laws from being adopted; it can only delay them. The present facade of the National Assembly was commissioned by Napoléon in 1807 to match the Greek style of the Madeleine across the Seine. Behind the National Assembly is the Place du Palais Bourbon. In the foreground is the Seine River.

## BOTANICAL GARDENS

(Opposite) Depicted here are the Paris Botanical Gardens (Jardin des Plantes) on the banks of the Seine. Behind them are the modern buildings of the Pierre and Marie Curie University.

## THE PALAIS DE JUSTICE

This complex on the Île de la Cité includes the Palais de Justice (the Hall of Justice), the Sainte-Chapelle and the Conciergerie. The Palais de Justice is on the site of an earlier Palace, once inhabited by Charlemagne. It was as early as the fifteenth century that justice began to be administered there, but the building did not become the Palais de Justice until the Revolution. The Conciergerie in the foreground, used to house the Concierge or administrator of the Royal Palace. It was during the Revolution that the Conciergerie played its most historic role, as a prison for some 2,600 aristocrats and others, who were later guillotined. Queen Marie-Antoinette spent the last thirty-five days of her life there before being beheaded on October 16, 1793. The Sainte-Chapelle in the courtyard of what is now the Palais de Justice is a thirteenth century jewel of stained-glass windows. At the right are views of the Palais de Justice, of the Conciergerie, and of all that is left of the Tour Saint-Jacques. Built in the sixteenth century, the Tour Saint-Jacques was one of the starting points for pilgrims on their trip to Santiago de Compostela. Today, it houses a meteorologic station.

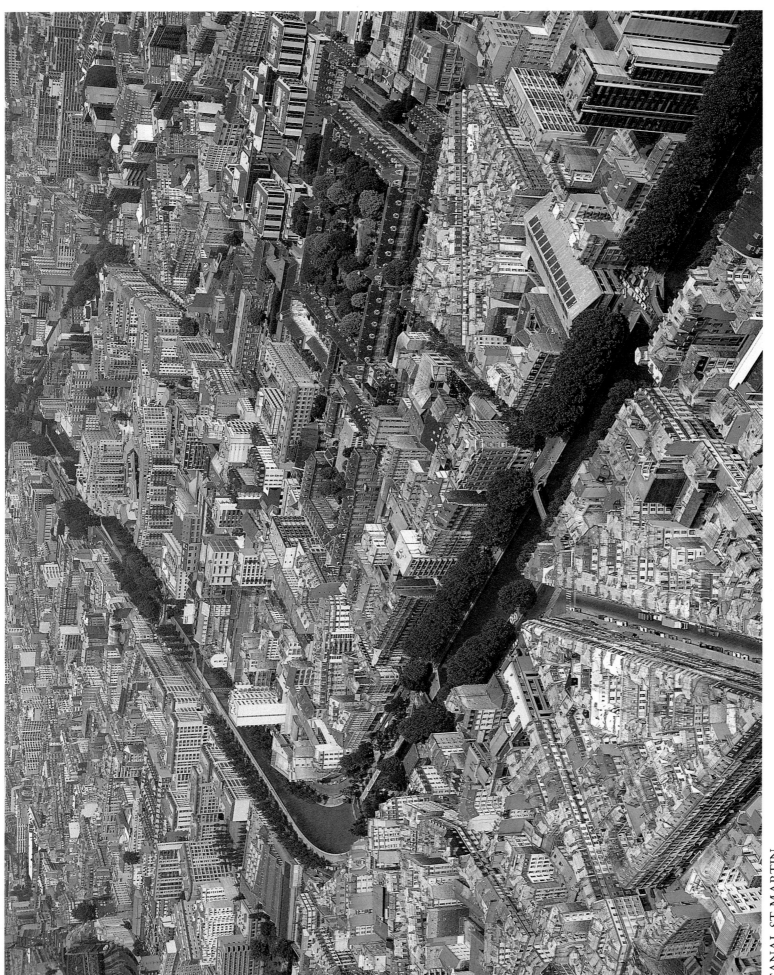

CANAL ST-MARTIN

The Canal St-Martin runs for about three miles from the Ourcq Canal to the Seine River. It is heavily travelled by some 4000 barges a year. On the far right is the St. Louis Hospital, built in the seventeenth century when Paris was hit by the plague.

THE ARENES DE LUTECE

(Opposite) The arena in the center of the picture is one of the few remaining signs of the Gallo-Roman occupation of Paris. There were several arenas on this site; thus, it is called the Arènes de Lutece. The arenas were destroyed in the third century B.C. and remained buried until 1869, when they were discovered during the building of a road. The arena above has been restored along with its ancient stone tiers which have been preserved.

ROTONDE DE LA VILLETTE

(Opposite) The Rotonde de la Villette is one of fifty-seven customs houses which composed part of a wall built around Paris between 1784 and 1791. The waterway in the foreground is the Bassin de la Villette. In the background is the Canal St-Martin.

THE PARC MONCEAU

Originally conceived of by the Duke of Chartres in 1778, the Parc Monceau is one of the more beautiful green areas of Paris. In the foreground is a rotunda, called the Pavillon de Chartres. Designed in the neoclassical style by the eighteenth century architect, Nicholas Ledoux, it is a rare survivor of the customs houses which surrounded Paris before the Revolution.

## BUTTES-CHAUMONT

It was once a garbage dump and a gathering place for tramps. Now the Buttes-Chaumont has been transformed into a beautiful 166-acre park, with a 5-acre lake which gets its water supply from the Canal Saint-Martin. The inauguration of the Buttes-Chaumont took place in 1867.

THE PÈRE LACHAISE

(Opposite) The Père Lachaise was purchased in 1626 by the Jesuits. It was Father de la Chaise, the personal confessor of Louis XIV, who erected the first buildings there. In 1763, the Jesuits were expelled. In 1803, the property was transformed into Paris' largest cemetery. During the revolt of the Paris Commune in 1871, the cemetery was the site of the bloodiest fighting. Among those buried there are the singer, Edith Piaf; the writers, Colette and Oscar Wilde; the composer, Georges Bizet; and the painters, Modigliani and Corot.

AVENUE DE L'OPERA—OPERA

In the foreground is the Avenue de l'Opéra, carved into the city in the middle of the nineteenth century. It is now one of Paris' streets of distinction. In the background is the Paris Opera—named the Palais Garnier after its thirty-five year old architect, Charles Garnier. Started in 1862, the Opera finally opened in 1875. The Paris Opera has the largest stage in the world which can accommodate 450 artists. The inside is dominated by a six-ton chandelier and a 1964 painting by Chagall which is on the ceiling.

## ARC DE TRIOMPHE

The Arc de Triomphe has always been an important point in Paris from which avenues branched off in many directions. It was not until 1758, that someone suggested building a monument there. An engineer, named Ribart, proposed building a giant elephant topped by a statue of Louis XV, with water gushing from the trunk of the elephant. It never happened. In 1806, just after the victory of the Battle of Austerlitz, Napoléon proposed building an arc of triumph to honor France's victorious armies. When Napoléon fell in 1814, the Arc de Triomphe was only partly built. The Arc was finally completed between 1832 and 1836. It was covered with

sculptures to illustrate the great moments of the French Empire and of the French Revolution.

These exceptional aerial photographs clearly show the avenues branching out of the Place Charles De Gaulle (previously named, l'Etoile—the Star) on which the Arc de Triomphe stands. Other than the Champs-Elysées, some of the more famous avenues emanating from the Arc are the Avenue Foch, the Avenue de la Grande Armée, and the Avenue Marceau, where one can see the Saint-Pierre-de-Chaillot Church.

## AVENUE FOCH

(Opposite) The Avenue Foch is one of the most beautiful avenues in Paris. It was created in 1854 and originally named the Avenue de l'Impératrice. Its purpose was to provide a particularly stately passage from the Étoile to the Bois de Boulogne. It is the broadest avenue in Paris. In 1929, it received its present name to honor the Maréchal Foch, a French hero of World War I. The apartments which line the Avenue Foch house the most wealthy of the Parisian population.

AVENUE MARCEAU

Avenue Marceau bends its elegant way from lower right to the Étoile where a frieze on the Arc de Triomphe depicts General Marceau's funeral.

MADELEINE

This view shows the Church of the Madeleine in the foreground. To the rear, on the left, is the Gare St. Lazare, the railroad station which links Paris to the suburbs and to Normandy. In the middle, on the right, is the roof of the Paris Opera.

## BOULEVARD DE LA MADELEINE

The Boulevard de la Madeleine is one of a number of "Grands Boulevards" or great boulevards in Paris. Originally traced in 1680, it derives its present name from the fact that it runs to the Madeleine Church, which is in the background.

## THE PLACE DU TROCADERO

(Opposite) The Place du Trocadéro, completed in 1858, is dominated by a statue of Maréchal Foch, the French hero of World War I. In the foreground are the Palais de Chaillot, built in 1937, which contains the Museum of Man, the Maritime Museum, the Henri Langlois Cinema Museum, the French Cinémathèque, one of the most complete and presti-gious film archives in the world and the People's National Theater, which seats 1,800 persons. Out of the Trocadéro flow arteries leading to the Alma bridge, the Arc de Triomphe, the Bois de Boulogne, and Porte Maillot, with its convention center, the Palais des Congrès.

## THE MOULIN DE LA GALETTE

(Opposite) The Moulin (Windmill) de la Galette, which dates back to the fifteenth century, stands in the middle of the Montmartre section of Paris. It served as an inspiration for many painters including Renoir and Van Gogh.

## PORTE MAILLOT

The Porte Maillot, on the west end of Paris, with the giant Palais des Congrès, is used as a convention center and also as a large hall for ballets, operas, and concerts.

## SACRÉ COEUR

On a clear day, you can see the Sacré-Coeur (the Sacred Heart) from 40 miles away. It stands at the top of the Montmarte district as a monument which dominates Paris.

After France's crushing defeat by the Germans in the War of 1870, the National Assembly, pushed by the important Roman Catholic lobby in France, decided, as a sign of hope, to build the Basilica of the Sacré-Couer. The design chosen produced a white church which looked like a huge wedding cake. Much of it was paid for by the public, that is, those of whom could contribute enough money to buy a stone, a pillar, or a column. Construction of the Sacré-Coeur began in 1875. Although it was officially dedicated in 1891, it was not actually completed until 1919. In 1895, a giant chariot pulled by more than 20 teams of oxen delivered the 19-ton bell, called the Savoyarde, to the church, where it was installed under the campanile.

The Sacré-Coeur has become a tremendous tourist attraction. It can be reached by walking up the long set of stairs to the church, or by taking the funicular which is to the left of the stairs. From the Sacré-Coeur, one gets an extraordinary view of Paris and of the Montmartre district, famous for its artists and outdoor cafés. Next to the Sacré-Coeur, one can see the smaller, beautiful church of Saint-Pierre-de-Montmartre, one of the oldest in Paris, as it was started in 1134.

SACRE-COEUR

(Opposite) This evening photo exemplifies the characterization of Paris as the "City of Light." In the foreground are lighted Bateau-Mouches, preparing for a trip down the river. In the background, bathed by the rays of the falling sun, is the Sacré-Coeur. To the right is the same scene in daylight.

MONTMARTRE
In the foreground of the Montmartre section of Paris can be seen the church of Saint-Jean-l'Evangéliste built between 1894 and 1904.

97

SIXTEENTH ARRONDISSEMENT

(Opposite) This view of the wealthy sixteenth arrondissement of Paris is seen with the Porte de St-Cloud in the foreground. On the left is the modern church of Sainte-Jeanne-de-Chantal. In the background, at the left, is the Longchamp race track.

BIBLIOTHEQUE NATIONALE

The national library (Bibliothèque Nationale) was moved seven times before it was finally installed in the Maison Tubeuf in 1720. It includes, today, nearly 9,000,000 volumes, among which are two Bibles printed by Gutenberg. It has collections of coins and stamps and the most important collections of prints and photographs in the world. Among the volumes included are books and manuscripts seized during the Revolution from abbeys, convents, and other ecclesiastical institutions. In the background are the gardens of the Palais-Royal.

99

## LA VILLETTE
La Villette was once the site of Paris' slaughterhouses. Under construction in this location is a museum of Science and Technology and what is to become the French capital's most important music hall.

## GARE DE LYON
(Opposite) If you are going south to the Cote d'Azur, you can catch your train at the Gare de Lyon, which has one of Paris' best restaurants, "Le Train Bleu." In the foreground is the Paris-Bercy Omnisports Palace, opened in 1983 by the municipality of Paris as a giant sports center. It has been the basis of one of Paris' strong arguments to be the host of the 1992 Olympic Games.

THE BOURSE DU COMMERCE
(Opposite) In the foreground is the Paris Commercial Exchange (the Bourse du Commerce) where commodity trading takes place. The present building, with its Rotunda, was erected in 1889 in the area of Paris which once included the wholesale produce markets. Les Halles, the markets, have since been moved to an area near Orly Airport. Massive con-

struction has been going on in the area for years. One of the works completed first was the Forum des Halles (in the background), a vast complex of shops and restaurants. Now under construction (in the center) is a huge complex which will include sports facilities, a hotel, and residential buildings, surrounded by gardens.

RITZ HOTEL

Here is a unique view of the esteemed Ritz Hotel in the Place Vendôme. Founded by Cesar Ritz in 1898, it is, today, the symbol of the elegance and of the style of the French luxury hotels. It has been lavishly restored by its new owner, Mohammed Al Fayed. Legend has it that the Ritz was "liberated" from the Germans by the American writer, Ernest Hemingway, at the end of World War II.

**BELLEVILLE**
Depicted is the modern Belleville section in the east of Paris near the Buttes-Chaumont.

**QUARTIER D'ITALIE**
(Opposite) Depicted here is the modern complex which has grown up near the Porte d'Italie in the southern sector of Paris. In the background, the Tour Montparnasse, the highest building in Paris, towers over the other structures.

# THE ENVIRONS

## VINCENNES

The Bois de Vincennes, the former Bondy Forest, at the left, was renovated under Napoléon III. It now contains a zoo, a race track, an amusement park, and a number of artificial lakes.

On the following page, stands the Royal Castle of Vincennes, the first part of which was completed in 1370. The Cardinal Mazarin, who became governor of Vincennes, added to the castle in the seventeenth century. During the Revolution, the mobs attempted to destroy the castle, but it was saved by the Marquis de La Fayette, a hero of the American Revolution. Napoléon converted the castle to an arsenal in the early nineteenth century and had the towers in the corners destroyed. On August 24, 1944, the day before the liberation of Paris, the Germans, who were occupying the castle, shot 25 resistance fighters and set off three mines which damaged the King's Pavilion and set fire to the Queen's Pavilion.

MEUDON

Near Meudon is France's most important astronomical observatory, created in 1876. The mushroom-like top was added in 1965. In the seventeenth century, Monseigneur, the son of Louis XIV, who owned a château nearby, hunted wolves on this property. The château, neglected after the French Revolution, was razed in 1804.

## LA DEFENSE

The decision in 1958 to transform a 2000 acre site, just west of Paris, into a new urban office and living area produced the largest construction job in the history of the Paris region. The results were: 30 skyscrapers, underground shopping centers, accesses to mass transit, and a number of colorful high-rise apartments (see photograph above). Some 50,000 persons work and live in La Défense. Their link to Paris is clear, as one can see the Arc de Triomphe in the background. Between the office building and the apartments is a park dedicated to the memory of the French writer, André Malraux. Among the buildings, stand statues produced by modern artists, such as Calder and Miro.

LONGCHAMP

The Longchamp race track was inaugurated by Napoléon III in 1857.
There was an abbey on the left side of the course, but, it was destroyed
by the Revolution. All that remains is the rebuilt windmill. Longchamp
is the site of Europe's most prestigious race, the *Arc de Triomphe*, held
each year on the first Sunday in October.

AUTEUIL
(Opposite) The Auteuil race track, on the edge of the Bois
de Boulogne, is the site of France's best steeplechasing.

113

BAGATELLE

(Opposite) Once the property of the French royalty, Bagatelle is now a beautiful garden inside the Bois de Boulogne.

THE RACING CLUB DE FRANCE

The most eminent sporting organization in France, the Racing Club de France, was founded in 1882. Its main facilities are in the Bois de Boulogne.

CERCLE DU BOIS DE BOULOGNE
The Cercle du Bois de Boulogne is a private club in the forest which specializes in tennis and skeet shooting.

NEUILLY
(Opposite) Neuilly-sur-Seine, to the west of Paris, is the richest of the city's suburbs.

## LA BOULIE AND SAINT-CLOUD

France has beautiful golf courses and has produced some international champions. On the left is La Boulie, the golf courses of the Racing Club of France. On the right is Saint-Cloud, the site of the annual French Open Golf Tournament which was being played when this photograph was made.

RENAULT
Founded in 1898, the Renault auto company has developed into one of the largest in Europe. Its principal plant in Billancourt, on the western rim of Paris, occupies both sides of the Seine and the Seguin island in the middle of the river. Thirty thousand people work there.

PARC DES PRINCES AND ROLAND GARROS
(Opposite) In the background is the Parc des Princes, Paris' largest sports stadium. It is the site of French and European soccer and rugby matches. In the foreground is the Roland Garros tennis stadium which is the site of the annual French Open, one of the four most important tennis tournaments in the world.

ECOLE POLYTECHNIQUE

(Opposite) The new and modern Ecole Polytechnique in Palaiseau is one of the two or three most highly respected schools in France. Polytechnique was founded in 1794 as a training ground for engineers destined to direct public works after the French Revolution. In 1804, Napoléon gave the school a military statute, and the training was expanded to include military engineering. Today's modern site is a far cry from the historic buildings which the school previously occupied in the center of Paris.

T.G.V.

One of France's most remarkable technological advances, the T.G.V. (Train à Grande Vitesse), whips through the French countryside at more than 200 miles per hour.

## ORLY-CHARLES DE GAULLE

On the left is Orly West Airport to the south of Paris. It is used almost exclusively for internal French flights. It was opened in 1971. On the right is Charles de Gaulle No. 1, a more recent airport north of Paris. This airport is reserved for international flights by foreign airlines. In the background, one can see Paris' latest airport, Charles de Gaulle No. 2, reserved exclusively for Air France national and international flights. It is from there that the Concorde leaves for its daily flight to New York.

# ILE DE FRANCE

CHAMPS

(Opposite) The eighteenth century Château de Champs, built by a French financier, is most noted for its gardens, considered to be among the most beautiful in France. Once the residence of the charismatic Madame de Pompadour, it now houses the work-shops where the treasures of French museums are restored.

ILE DE FRANCE

The region around Paris is called the Ile de France. Its classic beauty has been enjoyed since the time of the Celts.

Despite the ravages of the French Revolution, hundreds of castles, built from the twelfth to the nineteenth century, remain standing. Many of them, for example, Versailles and Fontainebleau, have become exquisite museums.

To visit the Ile de France is to experience some of the glories and grandeur of earlier times.

## SAINT-DENIS

The Basilica of Saint-Denis, which is located in a working class district in the north of Paris, was constructed in the twelfth century by the Abbot Suger. The Basilica was restored in the nineteenth century. At one time, it was the burial ground of kings, queens, and other royalty of France. But the tombs were desecrated during the French Revolution. Connected to the church is an ancient abbey, built in the eighteenth century and converted by Napoléon to a school for young daughters of members of the Legion of Honor.

## SAINT-GERMAIN-EN-LAYE

(Opposite) The Château Vieux de Saint-Germain-en-Laye was built by François I to control the roads to Normandy. Because Henri III was displeased with the Château Vieux, he built the Château Neuf only to have it destroyed later by Charles X. Today, the Château Vieux houses the National Museum of Antiquities.

## CHATEAU DE FONTAINEBLEAU

(Opposite) The Château de Fontainebleau, one of the largest royal residences in France, is deeply rooted in the history of the country. François I started building the castle in the sixteenth century. Subsequently, many other monarchs left their marks on Fontainebleau. Much of the original construction was completed by famous Italian artisans. It was here, at Fontainebleau, that Napoléon made his farewell speech to his troops in the Cour des Adieux, before being exiled on the island of Elba. And, it was here, in 1984, that the heads of state and the governments of the European Community met and finally resolved the European Economic Community's (E.E.C.) nagging budget dispute.

## MAISONS-LAFFITTE

The Château de Maisons-Laffitte was built between 1642 and 1651 near the Seine River. The opulent party, which heralded the opening of the castle, was attended by Louis XIV, when he was just thirteen years old. The Count d'Artois, the brother of Louis XV, bought the Château in 1777 and built the famous Maisons-Laffitte racetrack nearby. In the early nineteenth century, the Château became the gathering place for leading French political figures including the Marquis de La Fayette, a hero of the American Revolution.

131

## FERRIERES

The Château de Ferrières was built in the mid-nineteenth century by James de Rothschild, who was then the head of the French contingent of the famed European Rothschild banking family. Napoléon III attended the opening party there in 1862. Bismark lived at Ferrières while his German troops engaged in the siege of Paris during the War of 1870. In this century, it has been the site of lavish costume balls given by the Baron Guy de Rothschild and his wife Marie-Hélène. In 1777, the Rothschilds donated Ferrières to the Chancellery of the University of Paris.

## LES VAUX DE CERNAY

(Opposite) Les Vaux de Cernay, a twelfth century Cistercian Abbey, was partially destroyed during the French Revolution. In 1873, the property was purchased by the Baronne Nathaniel de Rothschild, who restored it to its present state.

PORT ROYAL

What is left of the Abbey of Port Royal des Champs, near Versailles, is more a memorial to new ideas than to old buildings. It was once a complex made up of an abbey and a school, which attracted the free spirits of the time. The most well-known of the students was the French writer, Jean Racine. Also attracted there was Blaise Pascal, a scientific genius of his era. The school and the abbey of Port Royal produced a theological, as well as moralistic, tempest in France which Louis XIV saw as a challenge to his influence. In 1709, the complex was closed. But, it still remains as a hallowed site for those who believe in the freedom of thought and of speech.

BRETEUIL

The Château de Breteuil was built over a period of three centuries and was finally finished in the nineteenth century. It has been in the hands of the Breteuil family since 1712 and can be rented for parties or picnics.

DAMPIERRE

The Château de Dampierre, built in 1680 on the site of a Renaissance palace, sits in a symmetrical garden designed by the famous Le Nôtre. The interior of the Château is considered one of the most beautiful in France, and it contains a royal apartment that was inhabited successively by Louis XIV, XV, and XVI.

GALLARDON

(Opposite) People have been waiting for more than 500 years for this tower, partly damaged in 1443, to collapse. But, what is left still stands and is called "L'épaule de Gallardon." The guide book suggests that you see it from as far away as possible. This aerial photograph is probably the best way to see this ancient oddity. Behind it is a church which was first built in the twelfth century, with further additions later.

**MORTEFONTAINE**

(Opposite) Once the home of Joseph Bonaparte and Caroline Murat, the Château of Mortefontaine and its beautiful surroundings also served as an inspiration to the great French painter, Corot, and to the celebrated French poet, Gérard de Nerval.

**RAMBOUILLET**

It was in the Château de Rambouillet, built in 1375, that François I died in 1547. Down through the centuries, many French monarchs came to this magnificent castle to hunt or to live. The English gardens of the castle were designed in the eighteenth century. It is from the Château de Rambouillet that General de Gaulle, who was living there from August 23 to 25, 1944, gave the orders for the final assault to liberate Paris. It was here that the first summit of the seven industrialized nations of the world took place in 1974 under the presidency of Valéry Giscard d'Estaing.

ROYAUMONT

Founded in 1235 by St. Louis, the Abbaye de Royaumont, minus its church which was destroyed during the French Revolution, is one of the many religious structures constructed by the Cistercians. It now belongs to the Royaumont Foundation and is used for seminars, study groups, and concerts. It has a superb garden, surrounded by the cloisters.

ECOUEN

(Opposite) Built between 1538 and 1555, the Château d'Ecouen now belongs to the French Ministry of Culture and houses the National Museum of the Renaissance. At one time, it was a school for the daughters of members of the Legion of Honor. The Château is an example of the architecture of the Second Renaissance.

ESCLIMONT (Opposite)

The Château d'Esclimont was built in 1543 for the Archbishop of Tours. The Renaissance facade was added in the nineteenth century. It is now a château-hotel.

VOISINS

This magnificent Château de Voisins, with its expansive, manicured gardens, its lake, and its river must have been a joy to the royalty who built it in the eighteenth century outside of Paris. It is so private, as it is surrounded by the trees of the thick forest. The architectural style of this massive structure is Neo-Grecian.

COURANCES

(Opposite) The surrounding forests, gardens, and ponds make the Château de Courances particularly attractive. It was built in 1550. In the nineteenth century, an imitation of the horseshoe stairway of the Château de Fontainebleau was added to the front.

ANET

What we see today is only a part of the spectacular Château of Anet built in the sixteenth century. Large portions of the Château were destroyed in the eighteenth century. It was built for Diane de Poitiers, a longtime mistress of Henri II.

## SENLIS

This city is one of the oldest in France and survived the days of the Romans and of the Barbarians. Senlis has the look of a fortress town, because the 350-yard Gallo-Roman fortification, which once surrounded it, has been replaced by houses.

The photograph above is a closer view of the Notre-Dame Cathedral of Senlis. Construction of this Cathedral started in 1153, just ten years before work began on the Notre-Dame in Paris. After being partially destroyed by lightning in 1504, the Notre-Dame Cathedral of Senlis was rebuilt in its present form.

## CHANTILLY

Chantilly is more than several castles and a beautiful race track; it is one of the most beautiful monuments to France's historic past. It is intriguing that the first castle was built there 2,000 years ago. The large Chantilly Château is a nineteenth century imitation of the Renaissance style. The smaller château is an authentic structure of the French Renaissance. Horse racing started there in 1834. The stables were built to house 240 horses.

Formerly well-known for its lace and porcelain manufacture and as the residence of the Condés, Chantilly is even more celebrated now for its château and the annual race of the Jockey Club. The park and the castle (now comprising an important museum) were bequeathed to the Institut de France by the duc d'Aumale in 1886 along with his library and art collection.

VÉTEUIL

The French painter, Monet, was so captivated by the beauty of Véteuil, that he lived there for three years. Situated on the Seine, its centerpiece is a church, started in the twelfth century, which took four centuries to finish. In older times, Véteuil was a village populated by wine growers.

149

ERMENONVILLE
(Opposite) Ermenonville, with its château, lovely lakes, and forests, is dedicated to the memory of Jean-Jacques Rousseau, France's celebrated philosopher. His tomb can be seen in the foreground of the picture. In 1794, his remains, like those of many other famous Frenchmen, were transferred to the Panthéon in Paris.

CHAALIS
Chaâlis is located near the Ermenonville forest. It was originally constructed as an Abbey in 1136. In succeeding years, it was virtually abandoned. Finally, in 1850, a woman bought it and transformed it into a castle, surrounded by superb gardens. Today, Chaâlis is the property of the French Institute.

## VERSAILLES

The Château de Versailles is the most striking reminder of the power and wealth of the French royalty in the seventeenth and eighteenth centuries. It is the place from which France was ruled for a little more than a century (1682 to 1789), by the Bourbon Dynasty. It was the fulfillment of a dream for Louis XIV. The building of Versailles took 22,000 workers and some of the best artists of the time. The construction lasted almost 50 years.

The complex is made up of the Château, its orangerie (orange grove), the Grand Trianon, the Petit Trianon, and more than 250 acres of lavish gardens. All of this has been mostly restored due to the work of its former curator, Gerald Van Der Kemp (now the curator of Giverny) and his American-born wife, and through contributions, for the most part, by Americans.

On the following page is a view of the Grand Trianon (part of Versailles), the favorite "country house" of Louis XIV, who liked to go there, sometimes by boat, with the women of his life.

On the left is an unusual view of the Versailles complex, behind the city of Versailles.

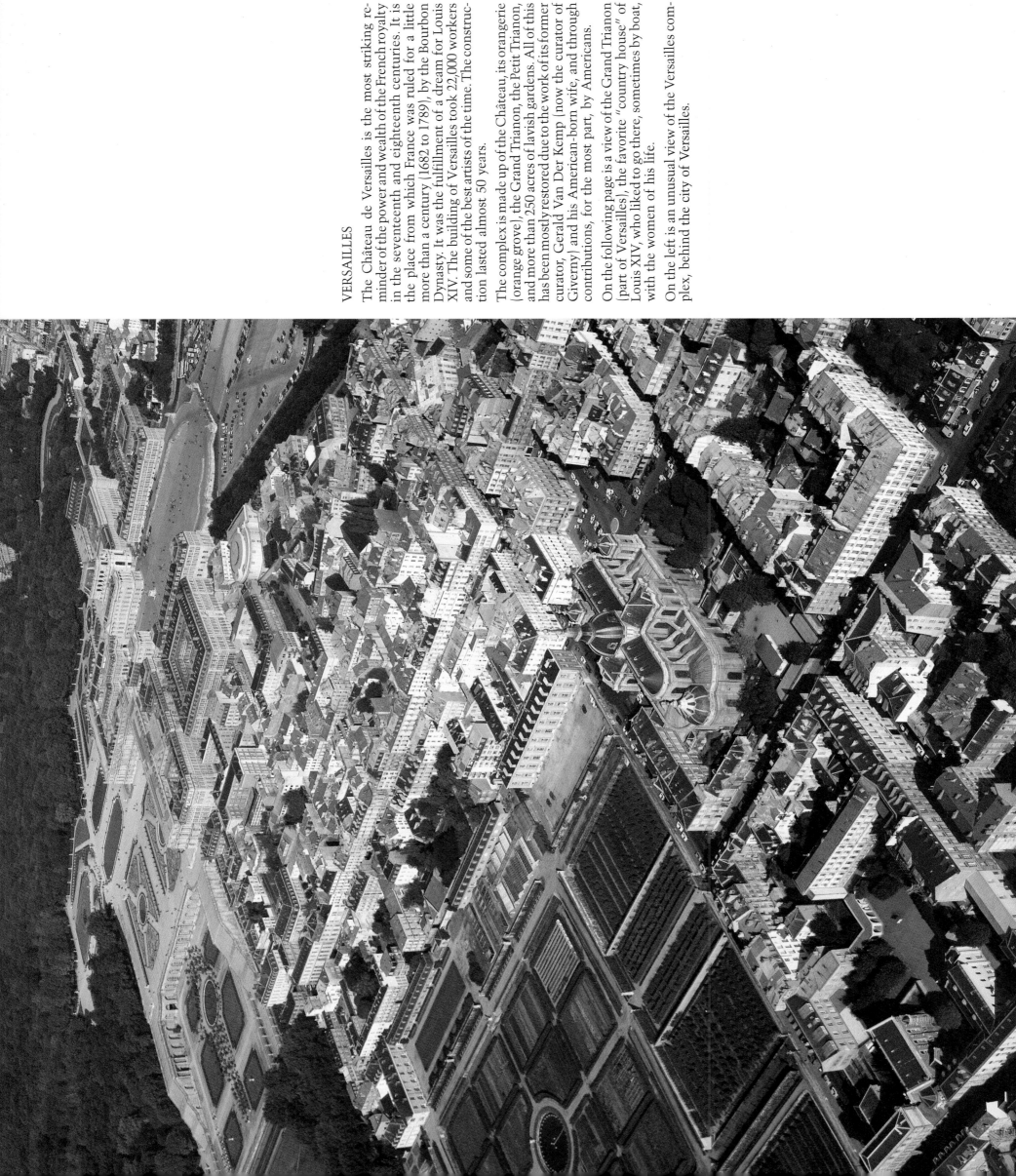

## GROS BOIS

The Château de Gros Bois, built under Henri VI and Louis XIII, became the home of the Maréchal Berthier during the Empire of Napoléon. Berthier decorated it with paintings depicting the glory of Napoléon's victories. The Château is a marvelous example of the mixture of stone and brick.

GRIGNON

The Château de Grignon was built during the reign of Louis XIII and restored under Napoléon. It is now the National Agronomic Center. It was
formerly called either the Royal School of Agriculture or the Imperial
School of Agriculture depending upon the preference of the person in
power at the time.

## LA ROCHE-GUYON

The Château de La Roche-Guyon was started in the thirteenth century. Building and rebuilding continued until its completion in the eighteenth century. The Château sits on the rise that comes up from the Seine River. Perhaps more interesting is the fortress behind it which was built in the eleventh century.

MER DE SABLE

You are only 30 miles from Paris, in the forest of Ermenonville, but, looking at it from the air, you would think you were over the Sahara Desert. Yet, this oddity, called Mer de Sable, is one of the favorite spots in France for young children who love riding on a small train which crosses the some 70-acres of sand. And, across the road, to add to the outing's entertainment, is a small zoo.

GIVERNY

(Opposite) The French Impressionist painter, Claude Monet, bought Giverny in 1890 after having lived there for some time. In 1914, he had a new studio built there. Many of Monet's paintings, including the *Water Lilies*, were inspired by these beautiful gardens. Giverny was recently restored and converted to a public museum with the help of a generous gift from Lila Acheson Wallace.

CREDITS

Bibliothèque Historique de la Ville de Paris
  Melle Hélène Verlet
  Mme. Marie de Thézy
  M. Jean-Marc Leri

and for the great cooperation of:
  M. Jean Derens

Musée Carnavalet
  Melle Françoise Reynaud

Caisse Nationale des Monuments Historiques
  M. Jean-Jacques Poulet-Allamagny

Musée Marmottan
  Mme. Marianne Delafond

Archives Nationales
  Mme. Nicole Felkay

Etablissement Public pour l'Amenagement de la Défense
  Mme. Catherine Le Morellec

l'Illustration

And for very special assistance from the
  Mme. Roxane Debuisson Collection.

BIBLIOGRAPHY

Dictionnaire des Rues de Paris—Jacques Hillairet
Dictionnaire de Paris—Larousse Publishers
Paris et les Parisiens—Robert Laffont Publishers
Histoire de Paris—René Héron de Villefosse
Construction de Paris—René Héron de Villefosse
Paris Histoire Illustrée—Gabrielle Wittkop,
                          Justus Franz Wittkop

Paris: a Century of Change (1878-1978) Norma Evenson
Paris—Henri Bidou
Paris Monumental—Flammarion Publishers
Michelin Green Guide on Paris
Paris aux Cent Villages—(monthly magazine)
Michelin Green Guide on Ile de France
Les Environs de Paris aujourd'hui—Paulette Crottès
Guide de l'Ile de France Mystérieuse—Tchou Publishers
Jardins de France—Ernest de Ganay
Hommage à Claude Monet—Catalogue of the Exhibition
                          at the Grand Palais, 1980

VAUX-LE-VICOMTE *(Photograph on page 5)*

It took 18,000 of the period's best artisans five years to build, what many consider to be, the most beautiful of the seventeenth century castles: namely, Vaux-le-Vicomte.

Fouquet, who had been prosecutor General of Paris, and later, the top assistant of Mazarin at the Ministry of Finance, built Vaux-le-Vicomte. Fouquet made the mistake of inviting King Louis XIV to a lavish party at his castle. The King became envious because his castle was less grand. He proceeded to arrest Fouquet and to take possession of Vaux-le-Vicomte. Not yet satisfied, he took the 18,000 artisans and had them build a sumptuous palace at Versailles to surpass the other castles. Fouquet's wife later succeeded in having Vaux-le-Vicomte returned to her. It survived the French Revolution with little damage and remains today, one of the privately-owned wonders of France.

MAINTENON *(Photograph on page 4)*

The Château de Maintenon, located four miles southeast of Versailles, was built in the fifteenth century on the foundation of a medieval fortress. It was given by Louis XIV to his second wife. The water in front of the castle flows in from the Eure River, and, in the foreground is located one of the most colossal projects of the period; that is, an aqueduct which was to be 5,000 yards long and 75 yards high.